Special-Day Sermon Outlines

Russell E. Spray

PULPIT LIBRARY

BAKER BOOK HOUSE Grand Rapids, Michigan 49506

To the memory of my father,
James Wesley Spray,
who always insisted he would
rather have me preach the
gospel than be president.

Copyright 1984 by
Baker Book House Company
ISBN: 0-8010-8241-2

Second printing, November 1987

These *Special-Day Sermon Outlines* are prepared without introductions and conclusions so that the speaker may use his own. They may be used by all who speak on spiritual themes. I pray that they will be a blessing to all who use and hear them.

PHOTOLITHOPRINTED BY CUSHING - MALLOY, INC.
ANN ARBOR, MICHIGAN, UNITED STATES OF AMERICA

Contents

1

How to Use Your T-I-M-E
(New Year's Day)

"But seek ye first the kingdom of God, and his righteousness; and all these things shall be added unto you" (Matt. 6:33).

I. T-ruthful Pursuits
"And ye shall know the truth, and the truth shall make you free" (John 8:32).
  A. Some Christians are less than honest in their daily pursuits. Their spiritual influence and outreach are hindered.
  B. Sometimes it is wise to remain silent. This is being tactful, not untruthful. Telling all may injure another's influence.
  C. Jesus Christ is the truth. We accept the truth, love the truth, and practice the truth when He becomes Lord of our lives (Eph. 4:15).

II. I-nvolved Efforts
"I must work the works of him that sent me . . . " (John 9:4).
  A. Many people shun involvement. Their self-centeredness causes them to avoid responsibility.
  B. Jesus was involved in the work of His Father. He healed the sick, helped the poor, and saved the lost.
  C. We must become involved in God's work by helping the less fortunate and sharing Christ with the unsaved (1 Cor. 3:9).

III. M-eaningful Action

"Remembering . . . your work of faith, and labour of love, and patience of hope . . ." (1 Thess. 1:3).

A. Life must have purpose and drive. Otherwise we become hopeless and helpless.

B. A feeling of accomplishment is a built-in psychological and spiritual need best fulfilled in Jesus Christ.

C. Meaningful action is found in working in the church, visiting the sick, helping the poor, and witnessing to the lost (Titus 3:14).

IV. E-ternal Values

"But lay up for yourselves treasures in heaven . . ." (Matt. 6:20).

A. Many are wasting their lives in temporal pursuits, loving possessions and sinful pleasures more than God.

B. We must give God first place. We must take time and make time to be holy.

C. Prayer, Bible reading, and sharing Christ with others hold eternal value (Matt. 9:37–38).

2

How to Be Optimistic

"Set your affection on things above, not on things on the earth"
(Col. 3:2).

Many Christians wonder if it is possible to be optimistic in today's world. We can be if we do these things:

I. Think About the Good
"*. . . think on these things" (Phil. 4:8).*
A. While Christians should be aware of the sinfulness in today's world, they should not dwell on the gloom and doom.
B. Thinking about the good brings optimistic thoughts. Positive thinking pleases God and others. It promotes personal well-being.

II. Look for the Good
"Looking unto Jesus . . ." (Heb. 12:2).
A. Many Christians look for the bad. They see only the faults and failures in others. They dwell on the negative side of life.
B. Optimistic Christians look for the good. They see the best in others and the positive aspects of circumstances. They keep their eyes on Jesus.

III. Listen to the Good
"*. . . faith cometh by hearing . . ." (Rom. 10:17).*
A. Millions listen to loud, lewd, lust-filled music on the airways. Filth dominates radio, television, and the movies.
B. We must listen to the good, hearing the voice of God as He speaks to us through prayer, Bible reading, and ministers.

IV. Talk About the Good

". . . talk ye of all his wondrous works" (Ps. 105:2).

A. Negative Christians complain and find fault continually. They discourage themselves, disappoint others, and displease God.

B. Optimistic Christians talk about God's goodness, graciousness and greatness. They are blessed and a blessing.

V. Work for the Good

". . . in every good work to do his will . . ." (Heb. 13:21).

A. Christians should not only think about, look for, listen to, and talk about the good, but they should do good.

B. We do God's work and please Him when we visit the sick and imprisoned, say kind words, give smiles, and share Christ with the unsaved.

VI. Go to the Good

A. Christians should protect their conscience and influence. They should avoid going to places that are questionable or morally degrading.

B. If we are faithful "to go" for God, He will be with us now and in the life to come.

3

Live It Up in 19— (New Year's Day)

While I live will I praise the Lord: I will sing praises unto my God while I have any being" (Ps. 146:2).

I. Laugh

"Then was our mouth filled with laughter, . . . The LORD hath done great things . . ." (Ps. 126:2).

A. Some Christians seldom laugh. They take themselves too seriously. Their lives are drab and unhappy.

B. Christians should develop a sense of humor. They should learn to laugh at themselves.

C. God's people should be happy people. They are forgiven, cleansed, and on their way to heaven.

II. Learn

". . . give me understanding, that I may learn thy commandments" (Ps. 119:73).

A. Some are unable to be the blessing they should be because they have limited their learning efforts.

B. If we are to give out, we must take in. The more we learn, the more we are able to learn. We should never stop.

C. Learning keeps one alive and happy. We should study God's Word and accept His revealed will for our lives.

III. Labor

"Labour not for the meat which perisheth, but for that meat which endureth unto everlasting life . . ." (John 6:27).

A. Boredom is often caused by lack of involvement. Those who have nothing to do are most unhappy.

B. Exercise and hobbies are helpful. Charity and hospital work are also commendable.

C. God's work is most rewarding. Church activities, praying for others, and personal soul-winning efforts are things that "endureth unto everlasting life."

IV. Love

". . . That he who loveth God love his brother also" (1 John 4:21).

A. Everyone needs to love and to be loved. Love is a built-in psychological need.

B. God's love never fails. His Word brings the assurance of His love to us.

C. God's love reaches out through us to bless and help others. It also lifts us to God's highest and our best. ". . . the greatest of these is love" (1 Cor. 13:13).

4

Have a Happy New Year
(New Year's Day)

"Thou crownest the year with thy goodness; and thy paths drop fatness" (Ps. 65:11).

I. Be Prayerful

"Be careful for nothing; but in every thing by prayer . . . let your requests be made known unto God" (Phil. 4:6).

A. Some think that praying makes no difference. Others simply forget, neglect, or fail to pray.

B. Prayer makes *all* the difference. God does things in answer to prayer that He otherwise would not do. Prayer changes things and people.

C. We must pray more this coming year. Prayer brings joy. It makes everything possible to those who believe (Eph. 6:18).

II. Be Positive

". . . whatsoever things are of good report . . . think on these things" (Phil. 4:8).

A. There is much negativism in today's world of sin, sorrow, and suffering. The news is mostly bad. It causes many to become pessimistic.

B. We should be aware of what is happening in the world without allowing it to darken and destroy our lives. We must look for the good.

C. Good things are happening, too. God is on the throne. Miracles are taking place (1 John 5:4).

III. Be Persevering

"... *watching... with all perseverance...*" *(Eph. 6:18).*

A. Troubles, trials, and testings will come to all this year.

B. It takes both bitter and sweet ingredients to make a cake, or to make a good life. The good and bad work together for our good and God's glory.

C. Keep on keeping on. Like the apostle Paul, we must be willing to suffer loss that we might win Christ. Exercise increases strength (Phil. 3:8).

IV. Be Productive

"With good will doing service, as to the Lord, and not to men" *(Eph. 6:7).*

A. Many Christians fail to work for God because they are interested only in selfish pursuits. They are unfulfilled and unhappy.

B. We should labor for the Lord. We find purpose in living when we lose ourselves in meaningful service for Him.

C. We do not find happiness by searching for it. It is a by-product, resulting from prayer, positive thinking, perseverance, and productive service for the Lord (1 Cor. 5:9).

5

Christ Arose (Easter)

"I am he that liveth, and was dead; and, behold, I am alive for evermore . . ." (Rev. 1:18).
". . . because I live, ye shall live also" (John 14:19).

I. That We Might Live in Him
"Therefore if any man be in Christ, he is a new creature" (2 Cor. 5:17).
- A. Because of Christ's death and resurrection we can become new creatures in Him, forgiven and cleansed.
- B. Our sins are forgiven when we repent and believe. When we give ourselves in total commitment to God, we are cleansed and filled with God's love (1 John 1:9).

II. That We Might Live Like Him
". . . leaving us an example, that ye should follow his steps" (1 Peter 2:21).
- A. Christ often prayed to His Father in heaven. He quoted Scripture to defeat Satan in times of temptation.
- B. Christ was kind, compassionate, understanding, and helpful to others.
- C. If we are to be like Christ, we must pray, read God's Word, be considerate of and helpful to the less fortunate (1 John 2:6).

III. That We Might Live for Him

". . . they which live should not . . . live unto themselves, but unto him . . ." (2 Cor. 5:15).

A. Many are unwilling to endure afflictions and persecutions for Christ. They follow selfish pursuits only.

B. We must work and witness for Christ, giving of our time, talents, and treasures.

C. Christ endured the worst, even death on a cross, for us. What are we willing to endure for Him (2 Cor. 5:20)?

IV. That We Might Live with Him

". . . and so shall we ever be with the Lord" (1 Thess. 4:17).

A. When Christ left this earth, He sent His Holy Spirit to abide with us forever (John 14:16).

B. The totally committed Christian is never alone.

C. When we leave this world we shall be forever with the Lord who has gone to prepare a place for us (John 14:2–3).

6

Christ's Death Can Change Your Life (Easter)

". . . I am the resurrection, and the life: he that believeth in me, though he were dead, yet shall he live" (John 11:25).

I. It Provides Pardon

". . . being now justified by his blood, we shall be saved from wrath through him" (Rom. 5:9).

A. Disobedience to God caused mankind to lose his first estate. It brought sorrow, suffering, and death to the human race.

B. Christ paid the penalty for our sins by His death on the cross. We are justified through His shed blood.

C. When we repent and believe we are forgiven and set free from the bondage of sin (2 Cor. 5:17).

II. It Promises Purity

". . . the blood of Jesus Christ . . . his Son cleanseth us from all sin" (1 John 1:7).

A. Today's morals are at an all-time low. Law, order, honor, and decency have been sadly neglected.

B. Christ's death brings purity of heart to the Christian. It can keep him cleansed—even in today's world.

C. A total commitment to Christ brings heart purity. Daily surrender brings continued cleansing (Heb. 13:12).

III. It Promotes Peace

"And, having made peace through the blood of his cross . . ." (Col. 1:20).

A. Today's world offers little real peace. Conflict, battles, struggle, and strife are everywhere.

B. Money cannot buy peace. Education cannot bring peace. Wars and treaties fail to effect lasting peace.

C. Jesus Christ gives peace in the midst of trouble. He made peace through the blood of His cross. He is our peace (John 14:27).

IV. It Produces Power

"But ye shall receive power, after that the Holy Ghost is come upon you" (Acts 1:8).

A. When Jesus left this world, He sent the Holy Spirit. The Holy Spirit indwells and empowers the totally committed Christian (John 14:16–18).

B. The surrendered Christian receives power for daily living. The Holy Spirit directs and guides him into all truth (John 16:13).

C. The Christian also receives power for service through the indwelling of the Holy Spirit, enabling him to share Christ with others (Acts 1:8).

7

How a Christian Mother Exhibits Love (Mother's Day)

"Her children arise up, and call her blessed; her husband also, and he praiseth her" (Prov. 31:28).

I. She Consecrates

"Commit thy way unto the LORD; trust also in him; and he shall bring it to pass" (Ps. 37:5).

A. A Christian mother yields herself to God, giving Him first place in her life.

B. She surrenders her children to God at birth. She wants His will to be done in their lives.

C. She continues to consecrate her children. She never stops. God's will must be done throughout their lives.

II. She Comforts

"As one whom his mother comforteth, so will I comfort you" (Isa. 66:13).

A. A mother's tender touch and kind words are most comforting to a child who is ill or discouraged.

B. A mother's caress and consolation soothe the fevered brow and bring hope to the troubled mind.

C. The comfort of a mother is likened to that of the Lord Himself. He is the greatest comforter of all.

III. She Counsels

"She openeth her mouth with wisdom; and in her tongue is the law of kindness" (Prov. 31:26).

A. A Christian mother understands the needs of her children. She is touched by the feeling of their infirmities.

B. Her children want to be near her. They feel at ease around her and they are proud to be seen with her.

C. A Christian mother encourages her children to talk to her. Her words of wisdom bring help to their areas of need.

IV. She Is Christ-like

"Now there stood by the cross of Jesus his mother . . ." (John 19:25).

A. When Jesus died upon the cross, His mother was there. She stood by her Son until the end.

B. Jesus gave Himself for us. He died for our sins, but He conquered the grave, and He lives today. He never fails those who come to Him.

C. A Christian mother will not fail her children. Like Christ she is willing to deny herself. She wants the very best for them because she is constrained by love.

8

A M-O-T-H-E-R Worthy of Praise

"Her children arise up, and call her blessed; her husband also, and he praiseth her" (Prov. 31:28).

Good mothers are unsurpassed blessings, exceeded only, perhaps, by Christ Himself. The following give some reasons why.

I. M-eekness
A. A good mother is humble before God. She praises Him for her children and for their accomplishments.
B. She petitions the Lord to protect and direct her children. Her utter dependence is upon God (Prov. 3:5).

II. O-ptimism
A. Despite adversities and setbacks, good mothers never give up on their children. A good mother keeps hope.
B. Her positive outlook inspires and lifts her children to their highest potential, to look for and expect the best (Ps. 121:1–2).

III. T-rust
A. Millions face the future with fear and frustration because they trust in temporal pursuits, possessions, and pleasures.
B. A good mother trusts in the Lord. Her faith and dedication encourage her children to face the future with assurance and confidence (Isa. 32:17).

IV. H-elpfulness

A. A good mother is not a hindrance to her children but a help. In sickness, discouragement, and setbacks, she comforts and shares with them (Isa. 66:13).

B. She also reaches out to help the needy, comfort the lonely, and share Christ with the unsaved as opportunity affords (1 Thess. 1:3).

V. E-ndurance

A. Many Christians throw up their hands in despair when adversity strikes. They lack endurance.

B. A good mother keeps on keeping on when there are mountains to climb, valleys to descend, deserts to cross, or rivers to forge. She endures to the end (Matt. 10:22).

VI. R-ewards

A. A good mother is rewarded in this life. The success of her children brings satisfaction and blessing.

B. She will be rewarded eternally for her meekness, optimism, trust, helpfulness, and endurance (Rev. 2:10).

9

Evidence of the Holy Spirit (Pentecost Sunday)

"For John truly baptized with water; but ye shall be baptized with the Holy Ghost not many days hence" (Acts 1:5).

I. The Downpouring

"And they were all filled with the Holy Ghost" (Acts 2:4).

A. Many Christians fail to make a total commitment of themselves to God. They hold certain areas of their lives in reserve.

B. To be filled with the Holy Spirit, one must surrender all to God—physically, mentally, and spiritually.

C. The downpouring of the Holy Spirit cleanses, fills, and empowers those who place themselves on God's altar unconditionally and by faith receive His fullness (Rom. 12:1).

II. The Uplifting

"... in the comfort of the Holy Ghost ..." (Acts 9:31).

A. Christians are subject to discouragements, hurts, and misunderstandings. Satan wants to defeat God's people.

B. Spirit-filled Christians possess a source of comfort and help that others do not have.

C. They are enabled to love, be kind, and pray for those who hate and despitefully use them (Titus 3:5).

III. The Indwelling

"... *he shall give you another Comforter, that he may abide with you for ever*" *(John 14:16).*

A. There are many lonely people in today's world. They are searching for fellowship, comfort, and love.

B. Those who love the Lord with their soul, mind, and strength enjoy His presence and reassurance.

C. Spirit-filled Christians are never alone. The Holy Spirit shall abide with them forever (John 16:7).

IV. The Outreaching

"*But ye shall receive power, after that the Holy Ghost is come upon you: and ye shall be witnesses unto me . . .*" *(Acts 1:8).*

A. Those who do not possess the fullness of the Spirit are limited. They often fail to work for God as they should.

B. The Holy Spirit brings courage and power to those who are totally committed to Him.

C. The yielded Christian is enabled to bring forth fruit by sharing Christ and witnessing to the lost (John 15:5).

10

The Infilling of the Spirit
(Pentecost Sunday)

"And when they had prayed . . . they were all filled with the Holy Ghost, and they spake the word of God with boldness" (Acts 4:31).

I. The Conviction

"But ye shall receive power, after that the Holy Ghost is come upon you" (Acts 1:8).

A. The first step toward receiving the fullness of the Spirit is realizing the need.

B. When we hunger and thirst after righteousness, the Holy Spirit is ready to cleanse our heart and fill us with His power and love (Matt. 5:6).

II. The Consecration

". . . present your bodies a living sacrifice, holy, acceptable unto God, which is your reasonable service" (Rom. 12:1).

A. Some Christians fail to surrender everything to God. They persist in clinging to selfish desires and questionable pursuits.

B. God's Holy Spirit is received by those who yield themselves unreservedly to God (Ps. 37:5).

III. The Claiming

". . . he that cometh to God must believe that he is . . . a rewarder of them that diligently seek him" (Heb. 11:6).

A. Some Christians feel the need to consecrate themselves to God, but they fail to appropriate needed faith.

B. We can receive nothing from God without believing. The infilling of the Holy Spirit is accompanied by faith (Acts 15:8-9).

IV. The Cleansing

". . . he is faithful . . . to cleanse us from all unrighteousness" (1 John 1:9).

A. Conviction, consecration, and faith bring the cleansing of the Holy Spirit.

B. As we daily continue to die to self, yielding to God, He continues to cleanse and fill us with His love. We are enabled to be a blessing to others and glorify God (1 Cor. 15:31).

11

Pentecostal P-O-W-E-R for Today

"But ye shall receive power, after that the Holy Ghost is come upon you . . ." (Acts 1:8).

Today's world is seeking power to protect themselves by destroying others. God's power is beneficial to mankind.

I. P-romised Power

"For the promise is unto you . . . and to all that are afar off . . ." (Acts 2:39).

A. God promised power not only to the disciples and Christians of that day but to "all that are afar off . . ." (Acts 2:39).

B. Christians who totally surrender and commit their lives to God are cleansed and endued with power by the Holy Spirit.

II. O-vercoming Power

"But Peter, standing up . . . lifted up his voice . . ." (Acts 2:14).

A. Before Pentecost, timid Peter denied Jesus three times. After he was endued with "overcoming power," he stood up boldly for Christ.

B. We must take our stand for Christ. When we are slighted, or persecuted, the Holy Spirit will enable us to overcome as Peter did.

III. W-itnessing Power

". . . and ye shall be witnesses unto me . . ." (Acts 1:8).

A. After Pentecost, witnessing became the method used by the church to win the unsaved and build Christ's kingdom on earth.

B. Witnessing is no less important today. God's power will enable Christians to share Christ with the lost and bring them into His kingdom.

IV. E-nduring Power

"Then Peter . . . said, We ought to obey God rather than men" (Acts 5:29).

A. The power of the Holy Spirit enabled the disciples to endure persecution, ridicule, and abuse for Christ's sake.

B. Today's world is filled with trouble and sorrow, but Spirit-filled Christians need not despair. Like the disciples, they can have enduring power.

V. R-ejoicing Power

And they departed . . . rejoicing that they were counted worthy to suffer shame for his name" (Acts 5:41).

A. The disciples counted it a privilege to suffer for Christ's sake. They were endued with rejoicing power.

B. Rejoicing power is available to totally committed Christians today. Like the disciples, we rejoice to be "counted worthy to suffer shame for His name."

12

The Qualities of a Good Father (Father's Day)

"Like as a father pitieth his children, so the LORD pitieth them that fear him" (Ps. 103:13).

I. Devotion

"The just man walketh in his integrity: his children are blessed after him" (Prov. 20:7).

A. A good father is devoted to his children. Confidence and understanding are encouraged through communication.

B. Children respond when they are free to express their joys and disappointments to a father who listens and cares.

C. We should be devoted to God our heavenly Father, giving Him our time, talent, and treasure. Fellowship increases our love to Him.

II. Discipline

"For whom the Lord loveth he correcteth; even as a father the son in whom he delighteth" (Prov. 3:12).

A. A good father corrects his children. They need the security that loving firmness brings.

B. Children are better able to please God later in life if they have learned obedience at home.

C. Our heavenly Father disciplines His children because He loves them. He knows what is best for them.

III. Direction

"Hear . . . the instruction of a father, and attend to know under-standing" (Prov. 4:1).

A. A good father offers direction to his children. Children often make quick and rash decisions. They need guidance and the right example to follow.

B. Children who accept instruction from their parents are better equipped to accept God's direction later in life.

C. Our heavenly Father wants to lead and instruct His children. Those who seek His will for their lives receive His guidance and direction.

IV. Diligence

"He that diligently seeketh good procureth favour" (Prov. 11:27).

A. A good father diligently seeks whatever is good for his children. His love demands the best possible for them.

B. Children are aware of their parents' love, concern, and sacrifice. It gives them security.

B. Our heavenly Father wants the best for His children. He loves and cares for them and is concerned about them.

13

A Worthy F-A-T-H-E-R

"Like as a father pitieth his children, so the LORD pitieth them that fear him" (Ps. 103:13).

In our world of declining moral values, good fathers are becoming harder to find. This message is designed to inspire fathers to meet God's challenge.

I. F-aithful

A. Today's society has been bombarded with unfaithfulness as has no other generation. It has compounded separation and divorce and destroyed millions of families.

B. A worthy father is faithful. He honors his marriage vows with utmost care. He protects his children and is loyal to them. He is constant in his allegiance to God (1 Cor. 4:2).

II. A-ffectionate

A. Many fathers are afraid to show affection. Their own insecurities cause them to forfeit untold blessings. Thus, happiness is denied to both themselves and their families.

B. Everyone needs to love and be loved. Fathers who show affection strengthen family ties and instill faith and security in their children (1 Peter 4:8).

III. T-rusting

A. Many fathers live with constant suspicion. Their children feel trapped and dominated, living in constant fear of what their parent will think, say, or do (Col. 3:21).

B. Trust is most important. It generates happiness, hope, and confidence. Parents and children who are trusting are better equipped to trust their heavenly Father.

IV. H-onorable

A. A good father meets his obligations promptly and is honest and respected. He diligently protects his family's name from slander and disgrace (2 Tim. 2:21).

B. His children have the utmost confidence in him and never have reason to question his integrity. His morals are above reproach in the sight of God and men (Isa. 43:4).

V. E-nergetic

A. A worthy father is not slothful or lazy. He works untiringly to feed and clothe his family and to make their future as secure as possible.

B. A good father also seeks to glorify God. He assists the less fortunate, comforts the bereaved and lonely, and shares Christ with the unsaved as opportunity affords (1 Thess. 1:3).

VI. R-ewarded

A. A worthy father is rewarded in this life. His children make him happy and are a blessing to others.

B. "His lord said unto him, Well done, thou good and faithful servant . . . enter thou into the joy of thy lord" (Matt. 25:21). Eternal rewards await the faithful.

14

How to Be F-R-E-E
(Independence Day)

"If the Son . . . shall make you free, ye shall be free indeed" (John 8:36).

I. F-aith (in God)

". . . Have faith in God" (Mark 11:22).

A. Many people are lacking in faith. Some are in bondage to the love of money. Some indulge in illicit and immoral sex. Others pursue excessive popularity.

B. Faith in God brings freedom from the bondage of sin. When we repent, surrender, and believe, we receive forgiveness and cleansing. We are set free (Gal. 5:1).

II. R-eliance (on God)

"Commit thy way unto the Lord; trust also in him; and he shall bring it to pass" (Ps. 37:5).

A. Many are insecure. They are in constant bondage to material pursuits, their own finite power, and other people.

B. Reliance on God brings freedom from the chains of insecurity. We can trust Him to supply all our needs. God is omnipotent (Phil. 4:19; Prov. 3:5-6).

III. E-nlistment (for God)

"... *The harvest truly is plenteous, but the labourers are few*" (Matt. 9:37).

A. These are busy times. Many are overwhelmed with the seeking of temporal and selfish gain.

B. We must take time for God, to help the needy, comfort the downcast, and share Christ with the lost. Doing God's work brings freedom from self-centeredness (Matt. 9:38).

IV. E-ternal Life (with God)

"... *I will come again, and receive you unto myself* ..." (John 14:3).

A. Many are fearful. They dwell on the gloomy side of life, failing to recognize that God holds the future.

B. Christians should be free from fear of the future—old age, death, and the judgment. These should not defeat us. We have the promise and assurance of eternal life with God (John 14:1–3).

15

How to Enlist Workers
(Labor Day)

*"Then saith he unto his disciples, The harvest truly is plenteous,
but the labourers are few" (Matt. 9:37).*

I. Get Them Interested

"Put them in mind . . . to be ready to every good work" (Titus 3:1).

A. Far too many Christians are unconcerned about the work of
God. They give attention to personal pleasure and possessions but fail to do God's work as they should.

B. These people need to be made aware of the need. We must
emphasize the importance, the lasting value, eternal rewards,
and spiritual blessings associated with doing God's work.

II. Get Them Informed

*"And let ours also learn to maintain good works . . . that they be
not unfruitful" (Titus 3:14).*

A. Many Christians do not witness for God because they do
not know how. They do not know where to go, when to go,
or what to say.

B. Workers must be informed. They should be trained not only
through words but by example, also. Experience brings
confidence.

III. Get Them Inspired

For we are labourers together with God . . ." (1 Cor. 3:9).

A. A lack of enthusiasm spells defeat in God's work as well as in secular work. Discouraged workers make poor witnesses.

B. Inspired workers are successful workers. Being aware of the virtues, value, and victory of working with God brings inspiration.

IV. Get Them Involved

"Pray ye . . . that he will send forth labourers into his harvest" (Matt. 9:38).

A. Christians lose a blessing when they do not get involved in God's work. They fail to lay up treasure in heaven (Matt. 6:19-21).

B. We must get involved personally. No one else can do the portion of work God has given each of us to do. It is what we do for Him that has lasting value.

16

How to Excel in God's Work
(Labor Day)

"Labour not for the meat which perisheth, but for that meat that endureth unto everlasting life . . ." (John 6:27).

I. Expound About God

". . . talk ye of all his wondrous works" (Ps. 105:2).

A. Too often Christians talk about the weather, their work, and their wants—possessions, positions, and pleasures—but they seldom speak about the things of God.

B. Christians should talk about spiritual values—the goodness of God, salvation, healing, and miracles.

C. They should witness to the unsaved, seeking to bring them to a saving knowledge of Jesus Christ (Acts 1:8).

II. Expend for God

". . . lay up for yourselves treasures in heaven . . ." (Matt. 6:20).

A. Some Christians are self-centered. They are generous with themselves but tightfisted with God.

B. If we are to excel in God's work, we must expend ourselves for Him—physically and financially.

C. When we willingly give God our best, He will reward us. We cannot outgive God (Matt. 6:33).

III. Expand with God

"He that abideth in me, and I in him, the same bringeth forth much fruit" (John 15:5).

A. We cannot remain stationary. We are either gaining or losing ground spiritually.

B. To excel in God's work we must grow in numbers as well as in faith and love.

C. We must meet the challenges of an expanding population. The gospel is for everyone everywhere (2 Thess. 1:3).

IV. Expect from God

". . . whatsoever ye shall ask in prayer, believing, ye shall receive" (Matt. 21:22).

A. Many Christians lack faith. They do not expect very much from God, and as the result, they do not receive very much from Him.

B. "According to our faith be it unto us." We shall receive about as much as we work and believe for.

C. Christians who expound, expend, and expand for God can expect from Him. They will not be disappointed (1 John 5:4).

17

God's Workmen (Labor Day)

"For we are labourers together with God: ye are God's husbandry, ye are God's building" (1 Cor. 3:9).

I. Perform God's Will

". . . he that doeth the will of God abideth for ever" (1 John 2:17).

A. Some never get to the place where they can accept God's will for their lives. They fear God will deal harshly with them.

B. Being in God's will is the best and most wonderful thing that can happen to anyone. His will always works for our good and His glory.

C. Through prayer and faith God will enable us to know His will. When we perform His will, we become workers together with God (2 Peter 3:9).

II. Proclaim God's Word

"For the word of God is quick, and powerful, . . . a discerner of the . . . heart" (Heb. 4:12).

A. Many Christians fail to know the Word of God as they should. Therefore, they fall short when it comes to sharing Christ with others.

B. The Word of God is the "sword of the Spirit." Without it, the Christian is like a soldier going to battle without a weapon (Eph. 6:17).

C. We must stand on the authority of God's Word, arming ourselves with it—learning it, loving it, living it, and laboring with it.

III. Practice God's Ways

"The Lord is righteous in all his ways, and holy in all his works" (Ps. 145:17).

A. Some Christians act more satanic than godly at times. Their influence, witness and outreach are limited.

B. God's ways produce the fruits of the Spirit—"love, joy, peace, longsuffering, gentleness, goodness, faith, meekness, temperance" (Gal. 5:22–23).

C. We must practice God's ways. Being holy and giving him first place makes us effective workers with God. (Zech. 3:7).

IV. Promote God's Work

"The harvest truly is plenteous, but the labourers are few" (Matt. 9:37).

A. Many Christians are busy promoting their own endeavors, indulging in materialistic and socialistic pursuits.

B. We must use a portion of our time, talent, and treasure to promote God's work, keeping earthly things in the right perspective.

C. We should keep eternal values in view by witnessing to and winning the lost to Jesus Christ (John 6:27).

18

Praise Brings Victory
(Thanksgiving)

"But thanks be to God, which giveth us the victory through our Lord Jesus Christ" (1 Cor. 15:57).

I. Praise the Lord for Everything
"Giving thanks always for all things unto God . . ." (Eph. 5:20).

A. Many people praise the Lord for the good and blame Him for the bad. They are filled with doubt, easily discouraged, and often defeated.

B. God sometimes allows difficulties to come our way to increase our patience and strengthen our faith. They should serve as stepping, not stumbling, stones.

C. Everything that God allows to come to us has been screened by His love and works together for our good. Praise pleases God and brings victory (Rom. 8:28).

I. Praise the Lord with Everything
"Praise him with the . . . trumpet . . . psaltry . . . harp . . . stringed instruments and organs" (Ps. 150:3–4).

A. Talents: Many Christians do not use their talents for God as they should. By failing to be a blessing to others, they lose a blessing themselves.

B. Treasure: Some people are lavish in spending for selfish endeavors, but they are tightfisted with God. We must give God first place by bringing His tithes and our offerings into His house.

C. Time: Most people have time for the things they really want to do. Christians must take time for God by sharing Christ with others and witnessing to the unsaved (Ps. 105:1–2).

III. Praise the Lord Through Everything

"In every thing give thanks: for this is the will of God . . . concerning you" (1 Thess. 5:18).

A. Most Christians praise the Lord when they are blessed with success, prosperity, and good health.

B. They should also praise the Lord when failure, loss, and ill health strike. Through it all Christians learn to pray, read God's Word, trust, and obey.

C. Christ gave His all, His very life for us. He deserves our praise. Praising God for everything, with everything, and through everything brings victory (Ps. 113:2–3).

19

Giving Thanks (Thanksgiving)

"Enter into his gates with thanksgiving, and into his courts with praise: be thankful unto him, and bless his name" (Ps. 100:4).

I. Thank God for What He Has Done

"The Lord hath done great things for us; whereof we are glad" (Ps. 126:3).

A. Disobedience brought sin and death to the human race. God provided righteousness and life through the death of His Son Jesus Christ. Many fail to appreciate what God has done.

B. The gifts of salvation, strength, serenity, and sustenance have been made available to us. They may be received by all who repent, believe, accept, and obey.

C. We should remember what God has done and thank Him for the many blessings He has given. Count them and name them one by one (Ps. 105:5).

II. Thank God for What He Is Doing

"Bless the Lord, O my soul, and forget not all his benefits" (Ps. 103:2).

A. Some people see only the bad and evil. They are immersed in trials and troubles, frustrations and futility. They are unthankful; therefore, they are displeasing to God.

B. We must take positive attitudes. Faith is pleasing to God. We must look for the good, the right, and the blessings of hope, faith, and love.

C. God is alive and still on the throne. He is working miracles in the lives of those who believe. We should be excited and thankful for what God is doing (Ps. 103:3–6).

III. Thank God for What He Will Do

"Fear not, O land; be glad and rejoice: for the Lord will do great things" (Joel 2:21).

A. Many people face the future with futility. They are discouraged and distraught about its prospects. They are limited by doubt and mistrust.

B. We must face the future with faith. "The Lord will do great things." He will make a way, supply our needs, and give strength and courage to all who trust Him.

C. The best is yet to come—eternity with the Lord. He is preparing a place for those who love Him. We should thank God for what He will do (1 Cor. 2:9).

20

The Value of Praise (Thanksgiving)

"Enter into his gates with thanksgiving, and into his courts with praise: be thankful unto him, and bless his name" (Ps. 100:4).

I. Praise Improves Your Faith

"Bless the LORD, O my soul, and forget not all his benefits" (Ps. 103:2).

A. Many people are weak in faith. They see little for which to praise the Lord.

B. When we praise God, we must think positive thoughts and disregard our doubts.

C. Faith is important. We cannot please God without it; therefore, Satan is constantly trying to dampen and diminish our faith.

D. Praising God breaks down Satan's defense and improves our faith.

II. Praise Inspires Your Hope

". . . hope thou in God: for I shall yet praise him . . ." (Ps. 42:11).

A. We cannot praise God and continue to be discouraged.

B. Praise works like magic to bring hope. When we praise, hope just naturally follows.

C. Jesus Christ is the hope of the world. Popularity, power, and possessions cannot meet our need, but He can.

D. When we accept Christ as Savior and Lord, we receive the joy of forgiveness, the peace of cleansing, and the hope of eternal life (Ps. 33:22).

III. Praise Increases Your Love

"... *let them also that love thy name be joyful in thee" (Ps. 5:11).*

A. Everyone needs to love and be loved. Love is a built-in spiritual and psychological need.

B. God is love, thus we receive love by receiving Him.

C. Praise keeps us from hostility and resentments. Hatred and strife do not mix with praise. Love increases as we praise Him.

D. Those who praise God in this life will also praise Him eternally (Rev. 19:1).

21

The Lord Is G-O-O-D

Scripture Reading: Psalm 107

"O give thanks unto the LORD, for he is good: for his mercy endureth for ever" (Ps. 107:1).

God is G-O-O-D. Let us consider some of His attributes. God is:

I. G-racious

"If so be ye have tasted that the Lord is gracious" (1 Peter 2:3).

A. The Lord is gracious. His mercy enables Him to forgive those who repent and believe. His compassion enables Him to comfort those who are bereaved and sorrowful.

B. Because of His thoughtfulness and good will, the Lord helps the needy and troubled. His love enables Him to care for and understand the afflicted, persecuted, and misunderstood.

C. We must be kind and compassionate. We must extend good will, do acts of thoughtfulness, and show favor toward others, emulating the Lord (Ps. 86:15).

II. O-mniscient

"Known unto God are all his works from the beginning of the world" (Acts 15:18).

A. Human knowledge is limited in spite of man's progress in science, psychology, and medicine. He has yet to learn how to live and die in peace.

B. The Lord knows everything. He knows about war, strife, and destruction. He also knows about peace, joy, and love. His knowledge is unlimited (Ps. 139:1–10).

C. Christians know the joy and peace of forgiveness and cleansing. They know that God will supply their needs and work everything together for their good (Rom. 8:28).

III. O-mnipotent

"Let every soul be subject unto the higher powers. For there is no power but of God . . ." (Rom. 13:1).

A. Many people attempt to accomplish everything in their own power and fail.

B. God's power is unlimited. Nothing is too difficult for Him. No sin is too great for Him to forgive; no suffering is too great for Him to heal; no task is too great for Him to do.

C. The Holy Spirit endues fully surrendered Christians with power, enabling them to work, witness, and win for the Lord (Josh. 1:5–9).

IV. D-urable

"The eternal God is thy refuge, and underneath are the everlasting arms . . ." (Deut. 33:27).

A. Our affluent society is acquainted with abundant possessions, but temporal things wear out, rust, and decay. Beauty fades. Youth vanishes. None of these are lasting.

B. In our frustrated world it is good to know there is One on whom we can depend. He never fails.

C. Christians should be spiritually durable. They should be trustworthy, dependable, and faithful. These shall enjoy everlasting life, for the Lord is good (Rev. 2:10).

22

Christmas Shopping (Christmas)

"Thanks be unto God for his unspeakable gift" (2 Cor. 9:15).

I. A Personal Gift

"For by grace are ye saved through faith . . . it is the gift of God" (Eph. 2:8).

A. Today's world offers little personalized attention. Mass production, computers, and electronics have all but eliminated the personal touch.

B. "Tailor-made" gifts should be the ultimate goal in gift selection. To find specific gifts for specific people we must consider their likes, dislikes, needs, and interests.

C. Christ is "made to order"; He is a personal gift. He becomes our personal Savior, bringing personal salvation, serenity, and security.

II. A Practical Gift

"Come unto me, all ye that labour and are heavy laden, and I will give you rest" (Matt. 11:28).

A. Many gifts are not useful. They are attractive and decorative, but serve little purpose.

B. Many people fail to repent of their sins and believe unto salvation. They join the church for social and economic reasons.

C. Jesus Christ is a practical gift. He alone can bring forgiveness and cleansing from all sin (Isa. 9:6).

III. A Pleasing Gift

"For he satisfieth the longing soul, and filleth the hungry soul with goodness" (Ps. 107:9).

A. Many gifts come from those with limited means. They may be sewn, created, or prepared with love and effort.

B. The most precious gift ever given took love, sacrifice, and death. It cost heaven's best—Jesus Christ, "chosen of God, and precious" (1 Peter 2:4).

C. Millions are longing for something to satisfy the emptiness of their souls. Jesus Christ is the answer for their need. He has solved more problems than any lawyer, salvaged more homes than any counselor, brought more peace than any general. He is a pleasing gift (Luke 3:22).

IV. A Permanent Gift

". . . I will never leave thee, nor forsake thee" (Heb. 13:5).

A. Many gifts are made with flimsy materials and faulty workmanship. They do not last.

B. Earthly treasures are temporal and fleeting. They wear out, corrode, and soon deteriorate.

C. Jesus Christ is a permanent gift. He gives everlasting life. We must receive Him, work with Him, witness for Him, and win others to Him (John 3:16).

23

J-E-S-U-S (Christmas)

"And she shall bring forth a son, and thou shalt call his name JESUS: for he shall save his people from their sins" (Matt. 1:21).

I. J-ustifying Jesus

". . . being now justified by his blood, we shall be saved from wrath through him" (Rom. 5:9).

- A. Mankind sinned, losing fellowship with God through disobedience. He deserved to die for his sins.
- B. Jesus gave His life on the cross, paying the penalty for our sins. All who repent and believe are justified and restored to fellowship with God (Rom. 4:24).

II. E-mancipating Jesus

"If the Son therefore shall make you free, ye shall be free indeed" (John 8:36).

- A. Moses was a great emancipator. The Israelites were freed from Egypt's bondage under his leadership. Abraham Lincoln was a great emancipator. Blacks were freed from slavery while he was president.
- B. Jesus Christ is the greatest emancipator of all. He sets men free from the bondage of sin (John 8:32).

III. S-anctifying Jesus

". . . we are sanctified through the offering . . . of Jesus Christ once for all" (Heb. 10:10).

- A. Some Christians fail to make a total commitment to God. They reserve certain areas of their life for selfish pursuits.

B. Jesus gave His life to sanctify those who surrender all to God. His Holy Spirit cleanses and fills them with His love (Heb. 10:14).

IV. U-niversal Jesus

"... *the Father sent the Son to be the Saviour of the world" (1 John 4:14).*

A. Prejudice and inequality abound in the world. Justice and fairness are lacking.

B. Jesus is not a respecter of persons. He forgives everyone who comes to Him—rich or poor, black or white (John 3:16).

V. S-atisfying Jesus

"For he satisfieth the longing soul, and filleth the hungry soul with goodness" (Ps. 107:9).

A. Many are seeking something to satisfy the emptiness in their lives—money, pleasure, and popularity.

B. Temporal things fail to satisfy the longing of the soul. Jesus brings peace, rest, and love. He never fails. He satisfies (Ps. 91:16).

24

The Gifts of Christ (Christmas)

"For the wages of sin is death; but the gift of God is eternal life through Jesus Christ our Lord" (Rom. 6:23).

I. Salvation

"Being justified freely by his grace through the redemption that is in Christ Jesus" (Rom. 3:24).

A. Jesus Christ brings forgiveness to those who repent and believe, releasing them from the bondage of guilt and sin.

B. The Holy Spirit cleanses and purifies the totally committed, filling them with God's love and empowering them for service.

II. Serenity

". . . my peace I give unto you . . . Let not your heart be troubled . . ." (John 14:27).

A. There is little peace in today's world. Trouble, sorrow, war, and strife abound.

B. Christ gives peace to those who trust Him as Savior and Lord. They receive His "peace on earth, good will toward men."

III. Strength

"I can do all things through Christ which strengtheneth me" (Phil. 4:13).

A. Sometimes Christians feel they cannot work for God. They lack the courage to witness.

B. We cannot do God's work within our own strength. But Christ gives power and courage to those who trust and obey.

IV. Stability

"But the God of all grace . . . make you perfect, stablish, strengthen, settle you" (1 Peter 5:10).

A. Many Christians are unstable and undependable. You never know where to find them. They are sometimes up and sometimes down.

B. Christ gives stability. Through prayer, faith, and effort we can become faithful, dependable Christians.

V. Security

"In my Father's house are many mansions. . . . I go to prepare a place for you . . ." (John 14:2).

A. Many place their confidence in temporal pursuits. Houses, land, cars, and televisions, etc., are finite and do not last.

B. Christ brings lasting security. He gives love, joy, and peace in this life, plus the joys of heaven in the world to come.

25

What to Do When Tragedy Strikes

"Casting all your care upon him; for he careth for you" (1 Peter 5:7).

I. Keep on Living

"I shall not die, but live, and declare the works of the LORD" (Ps. 118:17).

A. Christians are subject to tragedies like everyone else. Financial loss, failing health, and the passing of loved ones come to all.

B. When tragedy strikes, some want to lie down and die. They seek to escape by giving up.

C. We must keep on living by faith. When we continue to trust in the Lord and pray, we receive hope and help from Him (Ps. 37:5).

II. Keep on Lifting

"But Jesus took him by the hand, and lifted him up . . ." (Mark 9:27).

A. When Jesus was on earth, He went about doing good, forgiving sin, and easing suffering and sorrow. He is still the same today.

B. When tragedy strikes we overcome by doing things for others.

C. We minimize our own burdens by lifting the burdens of others. God helps us as we help others (Ps. 37:3).

III. Keep on Learning

"For whatsoever things were written aforetime were written for our learning, that we through patience and comfort of the Scriptures might have hope" (Rom. 15:4).

A. God has a purpose for allowing whatever comes to us. We should seek His reason.

B. Learning brings hope when tragedy strikes. We learn through promises, prayer, patience, and praise.

C. We must remember that everything works together for our good and God's glory (Rom. 8:28).

IV. Keep on Loving

". . . now abideth faith, hope, charity . . . but the greatest of these is charity" (1 Cor. 13:13).

A. Some withhold their love from God and others. They fear rejection or being hurt.

B. Our love is never given in vain. If it is rejected, it will return to enrich and improve our own lives.

C. Everyone needs to love and be loved. We cannot live without love. "God is love" (1 John 4:8).

26

The Everlasting Arms

"The eternal God is thy refuge, and underneath are the everlasting arms . . ." (Deut. 33:27).

In this atomic age it is comforting to know there is One who protects, cares, understands, and succors us in our hour of need. Friends, even loved ones, may let us down, but we need not fall, for "underneath are the everlasting arms."

I. The Everlasting Arms Lift Us Up

"Humble yourselves in the sight of the Lord, and he shall lift you up" (James 4:10).

A. Christians may feel discouraged at times, but they need not remain in the depths of despair.

B. "Why art thou cast down, O my soul? . . ." (Ps. 43:5). When the psalmist was distressed he immediately declared his hope in God, "who is the health of my countenance."

C. We must pray with humility and optimism, hoping in God. When we do we can rest assured that the everlasting arms will lift us up.

II. The Everlasting Arms Hold Us Up

". . . I will uphold thee with the right hand of my righteousness" (Isa. 41:10).

A. Many Christians have been hurt, disappointed, or let down by friends or loved ones. They need "the everlasting arms" to hold them up.

B. We must put our implicit trust in the Lord. We must depend on the everlasting promises of God. They will never fail (1 Peter 4:12–16).

C. God comforts us when we're lonely and bereaved. He loves us when we're mistreated. He holds us up when we have been let down.

III. The Everlasting Arms Keep Us Up

"Now unto him that is able to keep you from falling . . ." (Jude 24).

- A. Some Christians habitually neglect their personal devotions. Consequently they are up one day and down the next.
- B. Twentieth-century Christians are being tested as never before. ". . . the devil, as a roaring lion, walketh about, seeking whom he may devour" (1 Peter 5:8).
- C. We must remain steadfast in the faith. ". . . the God of all grace . . . stablish, strengthen, settle you" (1 Peter 5:10). Remember, "underneath are the everlasting arms."

IV. The Everlasting Arms Will Take Us Up

"We . . . shall be caught up together with them in the clouds, to meet the Lord in the air" (1 Thess. 4:17).

- A. For centuries millions of Christians have looked forward with great anticipation to going to heaven, a place where there will be no more sin, sorrow, and suffering.
- B. When Jesus left this earth, He promised to go to prepare such a place for those who love Him. He shall return and receive them unto Himself (John 14:1–3).
- C. The everlasting arms offer the best of both worlds. In this life they lift us up, hold us up, keep us up, and some day they will take us up "and so shall we ever be with the Lord" (1 Thess. 4:17).

27

What Is Your Life?
(Funeral Service)

". . . For what is your life? It is even a vapour, that appeareth for a little time, and then vanisheth away" (James 4:14).

I. A Time (Which Passeth Hastily)

". . . that appeareth for a little time, and then vanisheth away" (James 4:14).

A. Life is brief at the very best. Many save, hoard, and pinch pennies as though life will continue forever.

B. Material possessions will all be left behind. We should keep things in the right perspective.

C. We must give God first place in our lives. Only what we do for Him will have lasting value (Matt. 6:33).

II. A Task (to Perform Faithfully)

". . . be thou faithful unto death, and I will give thee a crown of life" (Rev. 2:10).

A. Life is not a mere playground. It is not to be wasted in sinful pleasure. Life is a task—a duty, a job, a work to be performed.

B. To be successful life must have meaning, drive, and purpose. This is found in the work we do for Christ.

C. We must help the less fortunate and share Christ with others, seeking to bring them into the assurance of salvation (James 2:14–17).

III. A Test (to Endure Courageously)

"Be strong and of good courage . . . for the LORD thy God is with thee whithersoever thou goest" (Josh. 1:9).

A. The test of faith comes to every individual. Each person must decide which way to take—the right or the wrong.

B. Those who choose the wrong way are destined to spiritual failure and eternal retribution.

C. Those who choose God's way are promised grace for trials, comfort in bereavement, and the hope of eternal life in the hereafter (James 1:12).

IV. A Trip (to Journey Trustingly)

"By faith he sojourned. . . . For he looked for a city . . . whose builder and maker is God" (Heb. 11:9–10).

A. Everyone is traveling. Life's road may be difficult at times with its mountains, valleys, floods, and tunnels.

B. God's grace is sufficient. He cares for His own. He never fails.

C. When we get to the end of the journey, the toils of the road will fade away. Christ will welcome us home, and we shall be forever with our Lord (John 14:1–4).

28

The Reach of Prayer
(World Day of Prayer)

"Pray without ceasing" (1 Thess. 5:17).

I. Prayer Reaches High

A. Just as a powerful telescope brings the planets into view, so prayer brings God near to the Christian.

B. Prayer reaches into the heavens, lifting the soul above the highest mountain, beyond the highest star.

C. The Christian never needs to feel fenced-in. Prayer can lift him through and above the clouds of darkness and despair. Prayer reaches high (Luke 18:1).

II. Prayer Reaches Low

A. Prayer reaches down to the lowest of the low. It extends to skid-row, into the slums and ghetto.

B. Prayer reaches lower than the stain of sin has gone. It reaches down to the drunkard, gambler, prostitute, thief, and liar.

C. Prayer is linked to omnipotence; it cannot fail. Friends sometimes fail; money fails; education fails; but Jesus never fails (Ps. 102:17).

III. Prayer Reaches Near

A. Prayer reaches nearer than breath itself. It reaches into the heart and soul to enrich and renew.

B. Prayer brings forgiveness, purity, and strength. It gives us compassion, love, and understanding for others.

C. Prayer can penetrate any situation—darkness, despair, and discouragement. It relieves tension, drives out fear, bringing peace, contentment, and victory (Ps. 55:16–18).

IV. Prayer Reaches Far

A. Prayer reaches out to the very limit of our need. There is no distance nor object that can hinder its reach.

B. There is no problem that prayer cannot solve, no burden that it cannot lift, no sin that it cannot forgive.

C. God does things in answer to prayer that He would not otherwise do. He reaches out to touch and help missionaries, friends, and loved ones around the world (Ps. 103:11–12).

29

When You P-R-A-Y

"But thou, when thou prayest, enter into thy closet, and when thou hast shut thy door, pray to thy Father which is in secret; and thy Father which seeth in secret shall reward thee openly" (Matt. 6:6).

When Christians P-R-A-Y, they will find that their prayers are more effective if they follow the following pattern.

I. P-raise

Enter into his gates with thanksgiving, and into his courts with praise . . ." (Ps. 100:4).

A. Many Christians are self-centered. They are only concerned with what they can get from God. They fail to praise Him as they should.

B. Christians should serve God for the right purpose. They should fellowship with Him because they love Him. Then His blessings and gifts will come to them.

C. When you pray begin with praise. Thank God for past blessings. Thank Him for present blessings. Thank Him for potential blessings (Ps. 113:3).

II. R-equest

". . . in every thing by prayer . . . with thanksgiving let your requests be made known unto God" (Phil. 4:6).

A. Some Christians have not because they ask not (James 4:2–3). Some try to bear their own burdens and fail. Others are simply neglectful and spiritually lazy.

B. We must bring our petitions to God—the little needs as well as the big problems. Molehills may become mountains if we neglect to pray about them.

C. God knows our needs before we ask, but He still wants us to ask in childlike faith. He does things through prayer that He would not otherwise do (Matt. 6:8).

III. A-ccept

". . . he that cometh to God must believe that he is, and that he is a rewarder of them that diligently seek him" (Heb. 11:6).

A. Christians often fail to receive from God because of their lack of faith. They want to receive first and then believe.

B. Faith is the Christian's means of receiving God and also receiving from God. Not only do some fail to receive (James 1:6–7) but they also fail to please God (Heb. 11:6).

C. The prayer of faith brings pardon, purity, peace, power, and provisions. God offers untold blessings to His believing children.

IV. Y-ield

". . . not my will, but thine, be done" (Luke 22:42).

A. Many settle for less than God's best because they fail to yield everything to Him. They hold some things in reserve for themselves.

B. Christ yielded His will to His Father's will, although it meant death on the cross. Christ's death paid the penalty for sin and brought salvation to mankind.

C. We must surrender totally to God's will. His will is always best. When we yield *to* God, He will enable us to yield *for* Him (Matt. 6:10).

30

The Rich Fool (Evangelistic Service)

Scripture Reading: Luke 12:16–20

"But God said unto him, Thou fool, this night thy soul shall be required of thee: then whose shall those things be, which thou hast provided?" (Luke 12:20).

I. His Diligence

". . . The ground of a certain rich man brought forth plentifully" (Luke 12:16).

A. The rich man knew how to bring forth a good harvest. He was a capable farmer.

B. God wants the best for His people. Prosperity is not wrong, but we must keep our possessions in the right perspective, giving God first place in our lives.

II. His Dilemma

". . . What shall I do, because I have no room where to bestow my fruits?" (Luke 12:17).

A. This man's prosperity presented a problem. Would he settle for selfish pursuits or would he choose to help others?

B. Each of us must make a similar decision. Will we be self-seeking, loving sinful pleasure and Satan, or will we show love, care, and concern for God and others?

III. His Decision

". . . This I will do: I will pull down my barns, and build greater . . ." (Luke 12:18).

A. The rich man chose the wrong way. While thinking only of himself, he forgot about others.

B. We must choose God's way. We must assist in the work of the church and help the less fortunate. We must always share Christ with others.

IV. His Delusion
"... *Soul, thou hast much goods laid up for many years; take thine ease ...*" *(Luke 12:19).*

A. This man stuffed his body while starving his soul. He thought more about the present than eternity.

B. Many Christians are too concerned with selfish and temporal pursuits such as making money and enjoying life's pleasures.

V. His Destiny
"... *Thou fool, this night thy soul shall be required of thee ...*" *(Luke 12:20).*

A. God called this man a fool. All his wealth was suddenly wasted and worthless. He made the wrong choice.

B. Which way are you choosing—good or evil, right or wrong, heaven or hell (Ps. 9:17)?

31

Presenting Christ Effectively

"Herein is my Father glorified, that ye bear much fruit; so shall ye be my disciples" (John 15:8).

Many Christians fall short when it comes to presenting Christ to the world. These four guidelines should help us present Him more effectively.

I. Be Sincere
"Now therefore fear the LORD, and serve him in sincerity and in truth . . ." (Josh. 24:14).
- A. One of the first requirements for successful soul-winning is sincerity. Our world is filled with shams but we must be "for real" if we are to present Christ effectively.
- B. God's love reaches out through us to "bear much fruit." There is no defense against a love that keeps on loving in an unloving environment.
- C. No mountain is too steep, no valley too deep for sincere love to reach. God's grace will be with those who are sincerely devoted to Him (Eph. 6:24).

II. Be Specific
". . . to him that ordereth his conversation aright will I shew the salvation of God" (Ps. 50:23).
- A. Many Christians are vague and indefinite when trying to present Christ. They talk in generalities and forfeit the opportunity to lead others to Him.
- B. The unsaved must be made aware that they are lost because all have sinned (Rom. 3:23). They must know from God's Word that Christ died to save sinners and that through faith they, too, can receive Him into their lives.
- C. We must be specific, bringing the unsaved to the point of decision. When they confess, repent, and believe in Christ, they are accepted into the family of God. Christ becomes their Savior and Lord (Ps. 51:13).

III. Be Scriptural

"For the word of God is quick, and powerful, and sharper than any two-edged sword . . ." (Heb. 4:12).

A. Many Christians fail when it comes to presenting Christ because they are not as well acquainted with God's Word as they should be.

B. In the Bible are Scriptures which can comfort the sorrowful and save the sinful. Effective workers read, study, and use God's promises.

C. We must present God's Word to all mankind. It is effective in meeting the needs of the rich and poor, the black and white, the high and low (Ps. 119:46).

IV. Be Spirit-led

". . . the spirit of truth . . . will guide you into all truth . . ." (John 16:13).

A. Some Christians are sincere, specific, and well-versed scripturally, yet they fail to present Christ effectively. They are not Spirit-led.

B. We must depend on the guidance and direction of the Holy Spirit. Finite power quavers, but God's infinite power never fails.

C. The Holy Spirit can direct us to the right person and give us the right words to speak at the right time and place. We are enabled to "bear much fruit" when we are sincere, specific, scriptural, and Spirit-led (Ps. 32:8).

32

Redemption—for All

"For God so loved the world, that he gave his only begotten Son, that whosoever believeth in him should not perish, but have everlasting life" (John 3:16).

This golden text has brought hope to millions. The simplicity of the gospel is the need of our world today. Christ offers redemption for all.

I. The Reason

"For God so loved the world . . ." (John 3:16).

A. Human love is limited in its outreach and extent. It is imperfect. None can make the sacrifice that God did (Gal. 1:4).

B. God's love is perfect and unlimited. It reaches out to every person, regardless of color, creed, or circumstance.

C. God's love forgives sins, cleanses hearts, heals hurts, and restores broken homes. The reason: God so loved the world.

II. The Ransom

". . . that he gave his only begotten Son . . ." (John 3:16).

A. Mankind sinned and deserved the penalty of death. God's love caused Him to pay the ransom. His Son died on the cross for our sins (Gal. 3:13).

B. We should glorify God by sharing His love with others. We should witness to the unsaved about the saving power of Jesus Christ (Rom. 3:23–25).

C. Salvation is God's free gift to all who repent and believe. It cannot be purchased or earned. The ransom: He gave His only begotten Son.

III. The Rescue

"*. . . that whosoever believeth in him should not perish . . .*" *(John 3:16).*

A. Faith is the means by which we are rescued from eternal death and hell. Everyone who believes in Christ may receive Him as Savior and Lord (Rom. 10:9–10).

B. Added blessings are also received by faith—peace of mind, purpose for living, and power for service.

C. Without faith we cannot please God or receive anything from Him (Heb. 11:6). The rescue: whosoever believeth in Him should not perish.

IV. The Reward

"*. . . but have everlasting life" (John 3:16).*

A. Many are seeking earthly rewards in personal gain and sinful pleasure. Temporal pursuits do not last; they will soon pass away.

B. Heavenly rewards are eternal. Jesus is preparing a place for those who love Him and will return to receive them unto Himself (John 14:1–3).

C. Our reward begins when we accept Christ, and it will never end. Not even death can separate us from the love of God (Rom. 8:35–39). The reward: everlasting life.

33

What to Do About the Less Fortunate (Missions)

". . . Inasmuch as ye have done it unto one of the least of these my brethren, ye have done it unto me" (Matt. 25:40).

I. Care for Their Pleas

". . . Thou Son of David, have mercy on us" (Matt. 9:27).

A. Many people turn a deaf ear to the cries of the less fortunate because they are selfish and unconcerned.

B. Jesus had compassion on the poor and needy. He healed the sick, gave sight to the blind, and forgave the sinful. He heard their cries.

C. We must listen to the pleas of others both far and near. We must pray for the sick, extend help to the poor, and love the unlovable (Matt. 10:38).

II. Bear with Their Deeds

"Sin no more, lest a worse thing come unto thee" (John 5:14).

A. Some Christians become impatient with the less fortunate. They sometimes take a "holier than thou" attitude toward them.

B. Christ was never a respecter of persons. He loved the sick, sorrowful, and sinful as well as the healthy, happy, and holy. He was ready to heal, comfort, and forgive all who came to Him.

C. We must empathize with the less fortunate. By putting ourselves in their place, we are enabled to bear with their deeds (Matt. 10:42).

III. Share in Their Needs

"For I was an hungered, and ye gave me meat . . ." (Matt. 25:35).

A. Many Christians fail to share with the needy of the world. Some are complacent. Some do not realize the magnitude and urgency of other's needs. Some are self-centered and unconcerned.

B. Jesus was never complacent or unconcerned. He lived and died for the less fortunate, bringing physical, mental, and spiritual life to them.

C. We must share in the needs of others, also. We must feed the hungry, clothe the naked, visit the sick, comfort the bereaved, and share Christ with the lost (Matt. 9:37–38).

34

As a Little C-H-I-L-D
(Children's Day)

Scripture Reading: Luke 18:10–17

". . . Whosoever shall not receive the kingdom of God as a little child shall in no wise enter therein" (Luke 18:17).

I. C-onfidence

". . . the confidence that we have . . . that, if we ask any thing . . . he heareth us" (1 John 5:14).

A. Children have confidence in their parents. They trust them implicitly to meet their needs.

B. Many grown-ups place their confidence in material gain or in other people. We should trust our heavenly Father to supply our needs (Phil. 4:19).

II. H-umility

"Whosoever . . . shall humble himself as this little child . . ." (Matt. 18:4).

A. A child is aware that he is small. He asks for assistance from grown-ups, depending on them for their strength and wisdom.

B. We must realize our weaknesses and inability to understand everything, too. We must ask the Lord for strength and wisdom (Ps. 27:1).

III. I-nvolvement

"Now then we are ambassadors for Christ . . ." (2 Cor. 5:20).

A. Children do not sit still very long. They are full of activity, often exhausting themselves in long hours of play.

B. We should become involved in God's work—attend church faithfully, assist the less fortunate, and share Christ with the unsaved (2 Cor. 5:14–15).

IV. L-ightheartedness
"Take . . . no [anxious] thought for the morrow" (Matt. 6:34).

A. Discouragement is short-lived with children. They are normally light-hearted and carefree.

B. Our heavenly Father wants us to be worry-free. He is able to bear our burdens and banish our fears (1 Peter 5:7).

V. D-etermination
". . . he that endureth to the end shall be saved" (Matt. 10:22).

A. Although a child falls many times while learning to walk, he never gives up or stops trying.

B. We must keep trying, too. In spite of failures and mistakes, we must persistently keep on keeping on. Faith is the victory (1 John 5:4).

35

Children Are People, Too

"Jesus said, 'Suffer the little children, and forbid them not, to come unto me: for of such is the kingdom of heaven'" (Matt. 19:14).

The wise man admonished, "Train up a child in the way he should go: and when he is old, he will not depart from it" (Prov. 22:6). Children need guidance and direction.

I. Children Are Thinking Something
A. Many children live in depressive, negative homes. These non-Christian abodes produce an unhealthy atmosphere—physically, mentally, and spiritually.
B. Homes must be kept alive with Christian love, hope, and joy. This influences children to be optimistic, to look for and expect the best (Phil. 4:8).

II. Children Are Seeing Something
A. Millions of children are wasting countless hours watching scenes of lust, filth, and violence on television and movie screens and are suffering untold harm.
B. Parents should choose with care the programs their children watch. Children must be taught to distinguish between the good and the bad, to look for that which is beneficial (Heb. 12:2).

III. Children Are Hearing Something
A. Many children listen to loud, lewd music and vulgarity filling the airways. In non-Christian homes and schools taking God's name in vain is not uncommon.
B. A child's faith is strengthened when he hears his parents read the Bible and offer prayers of petition and praise (Rom. 10:17).

IV. Children Are Saying Something

A. Babies learn to talk by repeating what their parents say. Children also repeat what their parents and others say.

B. Children should learn to speak wholesome words and recognize that foul, smutty, critical, unkind words do not indicate intelligence or common decency (Matt. 12:34).

V. Children Are Doing Something

A. Children cannot sit still long. They must be doing something, but they need discipline and direction to prevent them from being destructive.

B. Children should be taught to act constructively, to be respectful, helpful, and unselfish (Heb. 13:21).

VI. Children Are Going Somewhere

A. Many places of entertainment which are unconducive to Christian ideals are available to children. These should be avoided.

B. Children should be urged to attend wholesome church-related activities (Ps. 122:1). Going to the right places now may help lead them to the right place eternally.

36

How to Win the Young
(Youth Day)

"Let no man despise thy youth; but be thou an example of the believers, in word, in conversation, in charity, in spirit, in faith, in purity" (1 Tim. 4:12).

I. Love Them In (Don't Tune Them Out)
". . . see that ye love one another with a pure heart fervently"
(1 Peter 1:22).

A. Today, as never before, young people need love and understanding. They need to feel that they are wanted and needed.

B. Many churches have neglected their young people. The generation gap has caused a break-down in communication.

C. Young people are tomorrow's church. Christ loves them and died for them. Our prayers and love will go a long way toward mending, molding, and making their lives meaningful.

II. Lift Them Up (Don't Tear Them Down)
". . . for charity shall cover the multitude of sins" (1 Peter 4:8).

A. Young people are often criticized. Their hair styles, dress codes, and vocal expressions are sometimes harshly deplored. The bitter spirit of those who criticize is unacceptable to God. He looks on the heart of man.

B. There is only one God and He never changes. Humanistic methods, modes, and means are subject to change.

C. We can win young people by lifting them up, not tearing them down. Love makes the difference. It "covers the multitude of sins." Ours is a changing world. We must look for the good in it.

III. Lead Them On (Don't Turn Them Off)

"... *let us ... love ... in deed and in truth*" (1 John 3:18).

A. Young people flounder. They make rash and unwise decisions many times. They need guidance, direction, and love.

B. Christ is our example. He knew who He was, for what purpose He came, and where He was going. We should strive to emulate Him.

C. We should be a good example, guiding youth "in deed and in truth." With prayer, kindness, concern, and love, we can lead them on and win them for Christ.

37

The B-I-B-L-E

"All scripture is given by inspiration of God, and is profitable for doctrine, for reproof, for correction, for instruction in righteousness" (2 Tim. 3:16).

God's Word is powerful. It will do wonders for those who take time to read it, memorize it, and obey it. The B-I-B-L-E:

I. B-rightens
"Thy word is a lamp unto my feet, and a light unto my path" (Ps. 119:105).
   A. The Bible is a beacon, a lighthouse, transmitting warning signals and giving guidance. Its light shines through the darkness and storms of life to give encouragement and direction.
   B. The Word of God gives comfort to the bereaved and lonely, peace of mind to the troubled and distressed, and it helps those lost in the night of sin to find their way home (Ps. 119:41).

II. I-nstructs
"Order my steps in thy word: and let not any iniquity have dominion over me" (Ps. 119:133).
   A. The Bible teaches Christians the differences between right and wrong. Therefore, sin need not have dominion over them (Ps. 119:11).
   B. Sometimes Christians do not know what to do or which way to turn. Through God's Word they can receive strength and direction. ". . . I will guide thee with mine eye" (Ps. 32:8).

III. B-eautifies
"The LORD . . .will beautify the meek with salvation" (Ps. 149:4).
   A. The desire to be attractive is natural and healthy. Millions are searching for beauty through diets, cosmetics, treatments, and exercises.

B. The Bible provides the best answer for beauty. The beauty of Jesus is exemplified through good deeds, kindness, and understanding. It banishes pride, resentment, and strife (Ps. 96:9).

IV. L-iberates

"And I will walk at liberty: for I seek thy precepts" (Ps. 119:45).

A. Many Christians are in bondage to the opinions of others. They are afraid of losing approval and friendships.

B. The Bible points the way to freedom through Christ. We must seek His approval and do those things that are pleasing in His sight (John 8:32–36).

V. E-ndures

"For ever, O LORD, thy word is settled in heaven" (Ps. 119:89).

A. Few things are lasting—beauty fades; health deteriorates; wealth vanishes. Houses, cars, and gadgets wear out, rust, and decay.

B. Through the ages, the Bible has been misused and abused, but it still lives on. It brightens, instructs, beautifies, liberates, and endures (Matt. 24:35).

38

The Eminence of God's Word

"All scripture is given by inspiration of God, and is profitable for doctrine, for reproof, for correction, for instruction in righteousness" (2 Tim. 3:16).

The worth of God's Word is inestimable. It's value can never be reckoned. Among all other works, it holds first place. Its eminence is unquestioned.

I. God's Word Is Divine
"In the beginning was the Word, and the Word was with God, and the Word was God" (John 1:1).
A. Scripture refers to Christ as the Word—"was with God, and ... was God." The Second Person of the Holy Trinity took an active part in the work of creation.
B. Christ also came to earth and died on the cross, paying the penalty for the sins of mankind. He is divine (John 1:14).

II. God's Word Is Dependable
"For ever, O LORD, thy word is settled in heaven" (Ps. 119:89).
A. Books are read by the millions throughout the world. While many are good and helpful, many books are morally destructive and belong in the trash.
B. It is comforting to know there is one book that is dependable. God's Word has been tested, tried, and found true throughout the centuries.
C. We must read God's Word, remember it, and rely on it. It improves our faith, inspires our hope, and increases our love.

III. God's Word Is Dynamic

"The word of God is quick, and powerful . . . a discerner of the thoughts and intents of the heart" (Heb. 4:12).

A. God's Word is powerful, able, dynamic.
B. No burden is too heavy; no sorrow is too great; no valley is too deep; and no mountain is too steep. God's promises are sufficient whatever the need.
C. Salvation, strength, serenity, and sustenance await those who trust in the promises of God (1 Tim. 3:15).

IV. God's Word Is Durable

"Heaven and earth shall pass away: but my words shall not pass away" (Luke 21:33).

A. There are few things in today's materialistic society that are durable. Earthly possessions wear out, rust out, and deteriorate.
B. Christ admonished us to lay up treasures in heaven. These are permanent (Matt. 6:19–21). We do this by being faithful, helping those in need, and bringing others to a saving knowledge of Jesus Christ.
C. God's Word is durable. It endured the yesterdays. It endures today. And it will endure in the life to come.